THE DALLAS COWBOYS

BY THOMAS K. ADAMSON

EPIC

BELLWETHER MEDIA ★ MINNEAPOLIS, MN

EPIC

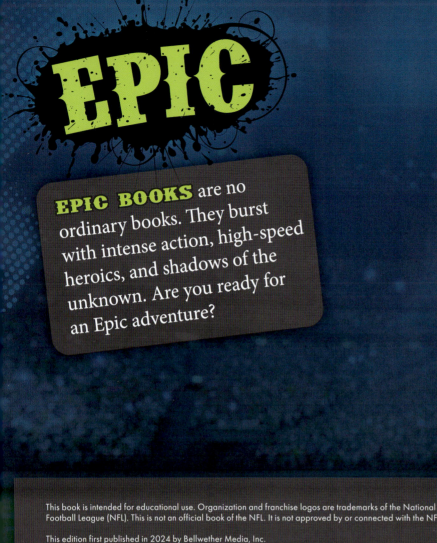

EPIC BOOKS are no ordinary books. They burst with intense action, high-speed heroics, and shadows of the unknown. Are you ready for an Epic adventure?

This book is intended for educational use. Organization and franchise logos are trademarks of the National Football League (NFL). This is not an official book of the NFL. It is not approved by or connected with the NFL.

This edition first published in 2024 by Bellwether Media, Inc.

No part of this publication may be reproduced in whole or in part without written permission of the publisher. For information regarding permission, write to Bellwether Media, Inc., Attention: Permissions Department, 6012 Blue Circle Drive, Minnetonka, MN 55343.

Library of Congress Cataloging-in-Publication Data

Names: Adamson, Thomas K., 1970- author.
Title: The Dallas Cowboys / by Thomas K. Adamson.
Description: Minneapolis, MN : Bellwether Media, 2024. | Series: Epic. NFL team profiles | Includes bibliographical references and index. | Audience: Ages 7-12 | Audience: Grades 2-3 | Summary: "Engaging images accompany information about the Dallas Cowboys. The combination of high-interest subject matter and light text is intended for students in grades 2 through 7"-- Provided by publisher.
Identifiers: LCCN 2023021299 (print) | LCCN 2023021300 (ebook) | ISBN 9798886874747 (library binding) | ISBN 9798886876628 (ebook)
Subjects: LCSH: Dallas Cowboys (Football team)--History--Juvenile literature.
Classification: LCC GV956.D3 A33 2024 (print) | LCC GV956.D3 (ebook) | DDC 796.332/64097642812--dc23/eng/20230508
LC record available at https://lccn.loc.gov/2023021299
LC ebook record available at https://lccn.loc.gov/2023021300

Text copyright © 2024 by Bellwether Media, Inc. EPIC and associated logos are trademarks and/or registered trademarks of Bellwether Media, Inc.

Editor: Elizabeth Neuenfeldt   Designer: Gabriel Hilger

Printed in the United States of America, North Mankato, MN.

TABLE OF CONTENTS

PRESCOTT'S BIG PLAY	4
THE HISTORY OF THE COWBOYS	6
THE COWBOYS TODAY	14
GAME DAY!	16
DALLAS COWBOYS FACTS	20
GLOSSARY	22
TO LEARN MORE	23
INDEX	24

PRESCOTT'S BIG PLAY

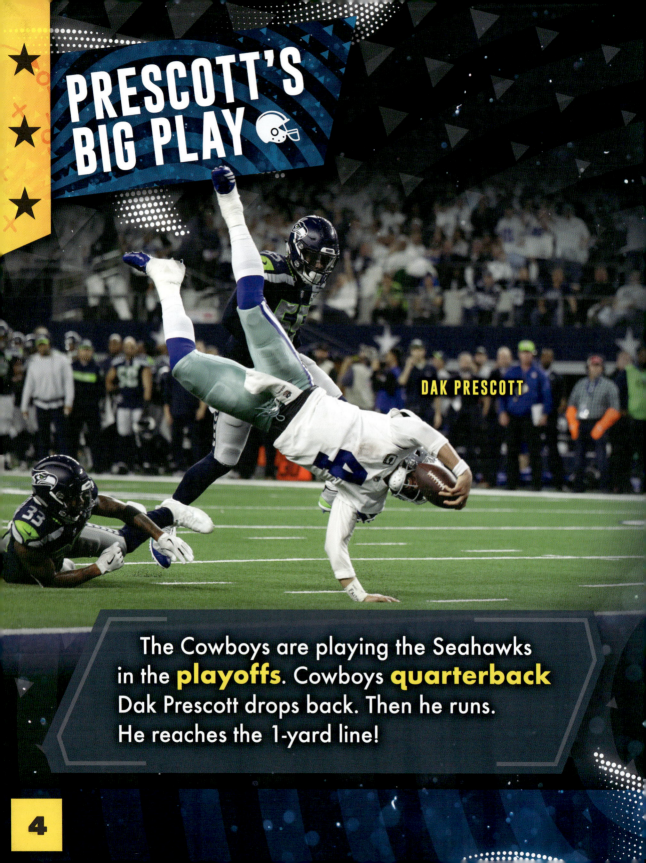

DAK PRESCOTT

The Cowboys are playing the Seahawks in the **playoffs**. Cowboys **quarterback** Dak Prescott drops back. Then he runs. He reaches the 1-yard line!

On the next play, Prescott scores! He helps the Cowboys win the game!

THE HISTORY OF THE COWBOYS

The Dallas Cowboys began in Texas. They joined the National Football League (NFL) in 1960. At first, the **expansion team** had little success.

In 1966, the team started a great record. They had 20 straight winning seasons under coach Tom Landry.

1960 COWBOYS GAME

THE ICE BOWL

The Cowboys played in the NFL's coldest game. In 1967, the temperature at the playoff game in Green Bay, Wisconsin, was −13 degrees Fahrenheit (−25 degrees Celsius)!

THE ICE BOWL

SUPER BOWL 6

In the 1970s, the Cowboys were a popular winning team. They reached the **Super Bowl** five times. They won twice!

SUPER BOWL 12

The Cowboys gained fans across the country. People started calling them America's Team.

The Cowboys struggled in the 1980s. Jerry Jones bought the team in 1989. He hired Jimmy Johnson as the new head coach.

JERRY JONES

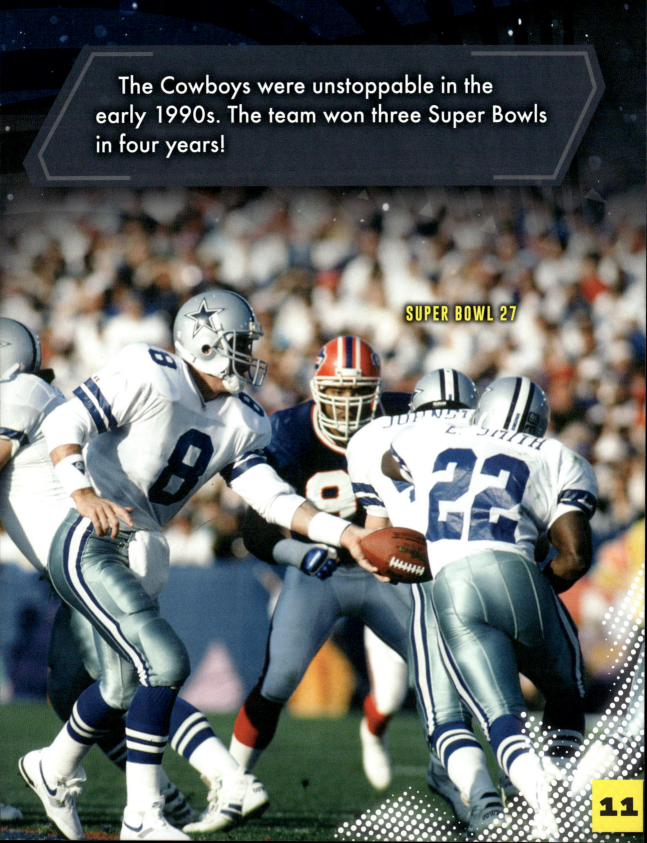

The Cowboys were unstoppable in the early 1990s. The team won three Super Bowls in four years!

SUPER BOWL 27

11

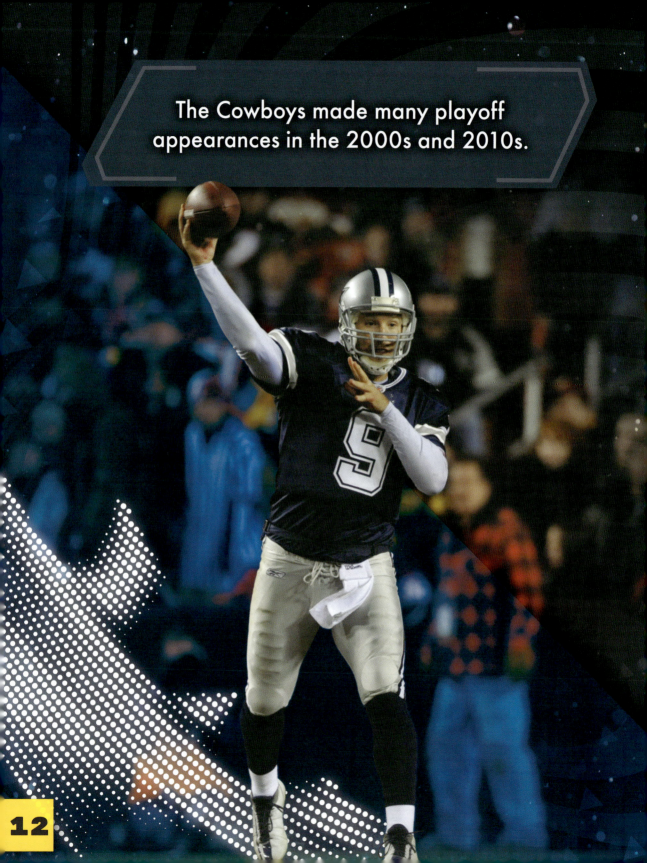

The Cowboys made many playoff appearances in the 2000s and 2010s.

In 2016, the team became the world's most valuable sports team. In 2022, it was worth over $8 billion!

🏆 TROPHY CASE 🏆

NFL CAPITOL DIVISION championships
3

NFC EAST championships
21

NFC championships
8

SUPER BOWL championships
5

THE COWBOYS TODAY

COWBOYS VS. EAGLES

The Cowboys play their home games in AT&T **Stadium** in Arlington, Texas.

The team plays in the NFC East **division**. Their biggest **rival** is the Philadelphia Eagles.

TEXAS-SIZED STADIUM
AT&T Stadium is the largest enclosed stadium in the NFL!

📍 LOCATION 📍

AT&T STADIUM
Arlington, Texas

TEXAS

GAME DAY!

The Dallas Cowboys Rhythm & Blue take the field after the team scores! This **drumline** and dance group began in 2009. It pumps up fans!

AT&T Stadium's huge video board hangs above the field. It gives fans a great view!

DALLAS COWBOYS RHYTHM & BLUE

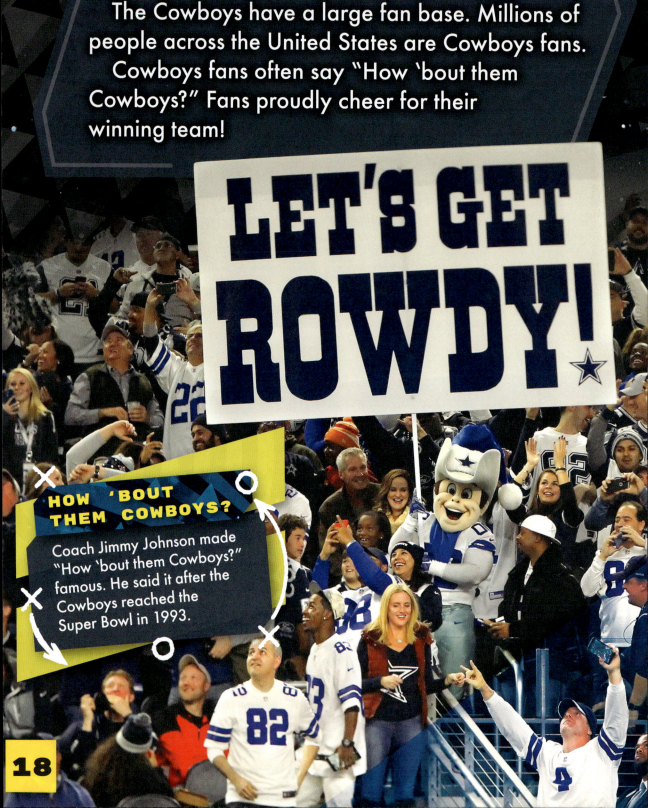

The Cowboys have a large fan base. Millions of people across the United States are Cowboys fans. Cowboys fans often say "How 'bout them Cowboys?" Fans proudly cheer for their winning team!

HOW 'BOUT THEM COWBOYS?

Coach Jimmy Johnson made "How 'bout them Cowboys?" famous. He said it after the Cowboys reached the Super Bowl in 1993.

★ FAMOUS PLAYERS

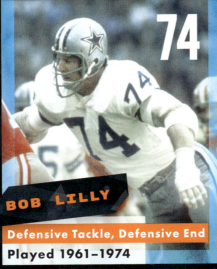

74

BOB LILLY

Defensive Tackle, Defensive End
Played 1961–1974

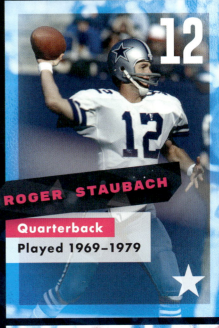

12

ROGER STAUBACH

Quarterback
Played 1969–1979

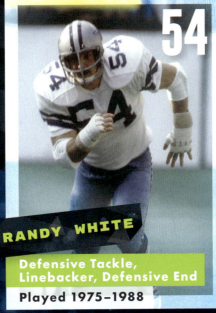

54

RANDY WHITE

Defensive Tackle, Linebacker, Defensive End
Played 1975–1988

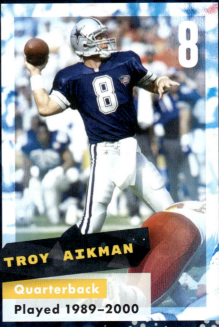

8

TROY AIKMAN

Quarterback
Played 1989–2000

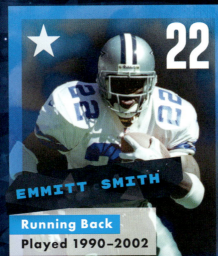

22

EMMITT SMITH

Running Back
Played 1990–2002

DALLAS COWBOYS FACTS

LOGO

| JOINED THE NFL | 1960 |

MASCOT
ROWDY

| NICKNAME | America's Team |

CONFERENCE National Football Conference (NFC)

COLORS

DIVISION | NFC East

 New York Giants
 Philadelphia Eagles
 Washington Commanders

STADIUM

★ AT&T STADIUM ★

opened May 27, 2009

holds **80,000** people

20

⏱ TIMELINE

1960
The Cowboys join the NFL

1996
The Cowboys win Super Bowl 30

1972
The Cowboys win Super Bowl 6

2016
The Cowboys become the most valuable sports team

2002
Emmitt Smith breaks the NFL record for most all-time rushing yards

★ RECORDS ★

All-Time Passing Leader	All-Time Rushing Leader	Single-Season Passing Touchdowns Leader	Single-Season Rushing Leader

Tony Romo
34,183 yards

Emmitt Smith
17,162 yards

Dak Prescott
37 touchdowns

DeMarco Murray
1,845 yards

GLOSSARY

division—a group of NFL teams from the same area that often play against each other; there are eight divisions in the NFL.

drumline—a group of musicians who play drums and cymbals, usually to pump up a crowd

expansion team—a new team added to a sports league

playoffs—games played after the regular season is over; playoff games determine which teams play in the championship game.

quarterback—a player whose main job is to throw and hand off the ball

rival—a long-standing opponent

stadium—an arena where sports are played

Super Bowl—the annual championship game of the NFL

TO LEARN MORE

AT THE LIBRARY

Abdo, Kenny. *Dallas Cowboys*. Minneapolis, Minn.: Abdo Zoom, 2022.

Morey, Allan. *Dak Prescott*. Minneapolis, Minn.: Bellwether Media, 2023.

Whiting, Jim. *Dallas Cowboys*. Mankato, Minn.: The Creative Company, 2020.

ON THE WEB

FACTSURFER

Factsurfer.com gives you a safe, fun way to find more information.

1. Go to www.factsurfer.com.

2. Enter "Dallas Cowboys" into the search box and click 🔍.

3. Select your book cover to see a list of related content.

INDEX

Arlington, Texas, 14, 15
AT&T Stadium, 14, 15, 16, 17, 20
colors, 20
Dallas Cowboys facts, 20–21
Dallas Cowboys Rhythm & Blue, 16
expansion team, 6
famous players, 19
fans, 9, 16, 18
history, 4, 5, 6, 7, 8, 9, 10, 11, 12, 13, 16, 18
Ice Bowl, 7
Johnson, Jimmy, 10, 18
Jones, Jerry, 10
Landry, Tom, 6

mascot, 20
National Football League (NFL), 6, 7, 15, 20
NFC East, 15, 20
nickname, 9, 20
playoffs, 4, 5, 7, 12
positions, 4
Prescott, Dak, 4, 5
records, 21
rival, 15
Super Bowl, 8, 9, 11, 18
Texas, 6
timeline, 21
trophy case, 13
value, 13

The images in this book are reproduced through the courtesy of: James D. Smith/ AP Images, cover; Dorti, cover (stadium); Kim McIsaac/ Contributor/ Getty, p. 3; Ton Hauck/ Contributor/ Getty, p. 4; Ron Jenkins/ AP Images, p. 5; ASSOCIATED PRESS/ AP Images, p. 6; Vernon J. Biever/ AP Images, pp. 6-7; Tony Tomsic/ AP Images, p. 8; Peter Read Miller/ AP Images, p. 9; Eric Gay/ AP Images, p. 10; Paul Spinelli/ AP Images, pp. 10-11; Larry French/ Stringer/ Getty, p. 12; Cooper Neill/ Contributor/ Getty, p. 14; Katherine Welles, p. 15 (AT&T Stadium); NFL/ Wikipedia, pp. 15 (Dallas Cowboys logo), 20 (Cowboys logo, Giants logo, Eagles logo, Commanders logo, NFC logo); Sharon Ellman/ AP Images, p. 16; Roger Steinman/ AP Images, pp. 16-17; Icon Sportswire/ Contributor/ Getty, pp. 18-19; Focus On Sport/ Contributor/ Getty, pp. 19 (Bob Lily, Roger Staubach, Randy White, Troy Aikman), 21 (1972, Emmitt Smith); Jamie Squire/ Staff/ Getty, p. 19 (Emmitt Smith); ZUMA Press, Inc./ Alamy, p. 20 (mascot); Jed Jacobsohn/ Staff/ Getty, p. 20 (stadium); Robert Riger/ Contributor/ Getty, p. 21 (1960); Al Bello/ Staff/ Getty, p. 21 (1996); Fort Worth Star-Telegram/ Contributor/ Getty, p. 21 (2002); Tom Pennington/ Staff/ Getty, p. 21 (2016); Wesley Hitt/ Contributor/ Getty, p. 21 (Tony Romo); NurPhoto SRL/ Alamy, p. 21 (Dak Prescott); Frederick Breedon/ Contributor/ Getty, p. 21 (DeMarco Murray); Sam Hodde/ Stringer/ Getty, p. 23.